BASEBALL TIME!

by Brendan Flynn

BUMBA BOOKS™

LERNER PUBLICATIONS ◆ MINNEAPOLIS

Note to Educators:

Throughout this book, you'll find critical thinking questions. These can be used to engage young readers in thinking critically about the topic and in using the text and photos to do so.

Lerner Publications Company
A division of Lerner Publishing Group, Inc.
241 First Avenue North
Minneapolis, MN 55401 USA

For reading levels and more information, look up this title at www.lernerbooks.com.

Library of Congress Cataloging-in-Publication Data

Names: Flynn, Brendan, 1968–
Title: Baseball time! / by Brendan Flynn.
Description: Minneapolis : Lerner Publications, [2016] | 2017. | Series: Bumba books—Sports Time! | Includes index.
Identifiers: LCCN 2015048784 (print) | LCCN 2015050404 (ebook) | ISBN 9781512414318 (lb : alk. paper) | ISBN 9781512415377 (pb : alk. paper) | ISBN 9781512415384 (eb pdf)
Subjects: LCSH: Baseball—Juvenile literature.
Classification: LCC GV867.5 .F59 2016 (print) | LCC GV867.5 (ebook) | DDC 796.357—dc23

LC record available at http://lccn.loc.gov/2015048784

Manufactured in the United States of America
1 – VP – 7/15/16

LERNER

SOURCE

Expand learning beyond the printed book. Download free, complementary educational resources for this book from our website, www.lerneresource.com.

Table of
Contents

We Play Baseball

Baseball is a fun game.

People play this sport in summer.

bat

ball

glove

6

You need a bat.

You need a ball.

You need a glove.

The infield is dirt.

There are four bases.

The outfield is grass.

Which part of the field are the bases in?

Two teams play each other.

One team starts in the field.

The other team bats.

The pitcher throws

the ball.

The batter swings the bat.

He hits the ball.

He runs to first base.

Why does the
batter wear
a helmet?

Fielders try to catch the ball.

They can also tag the batter with the ball.

Then the batter is out.

Teams change sides after three outs.

Why do fielders wear gloves?

A player goes around all

the bases.

This is a run.

The team with the most runs wins.

You can watch baseball at a park.

You can see games on TV too.

Players and fans can have a fun day at the ballpark.

Baseball Field

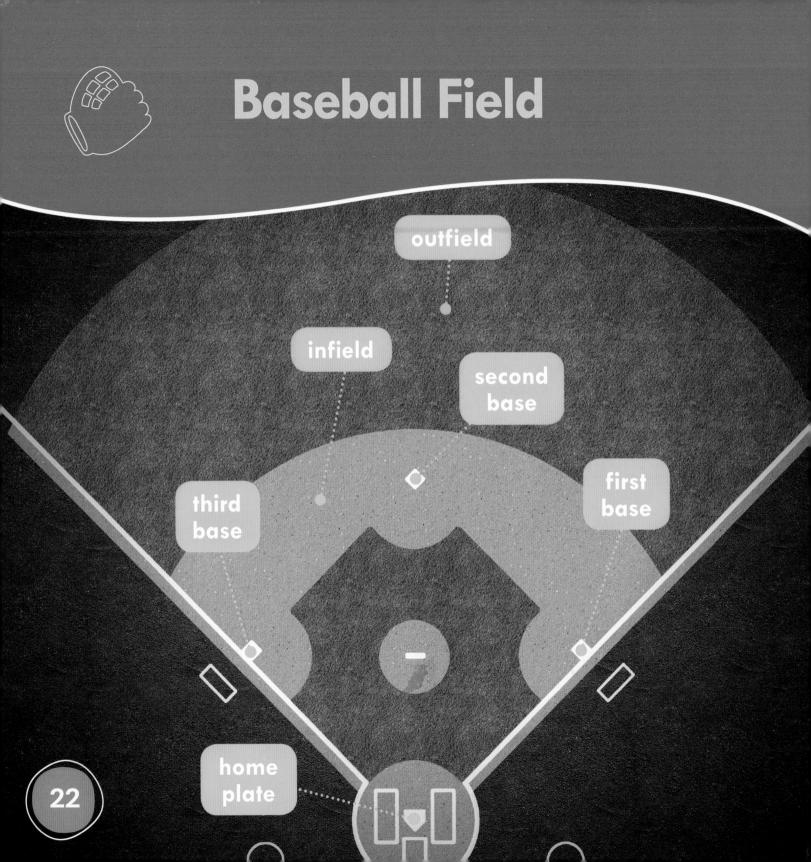

outfield

infield

second base

third base

first base

home plate

Picture Glossary

bases

four spots in the infield where the runner runs to

fielders

players who try to get the batter out

infield

the part of the field with dirt

outfield

the part of the field with grass

Index

Read More

Berne, Emma Carlson. *What's Your Story, Jackie Robinson?* Minneapolis: Lerner Publications, 2016.

Morey, Allan. *Baseball.* Minneapolis: Bullfrog Books, 2015.

Nelson, Robin. *Baseball Is Fun!* Minneapolis: Lerner Publications, 2014.

Photo Credits